50 of The Greatest Coloring Pages

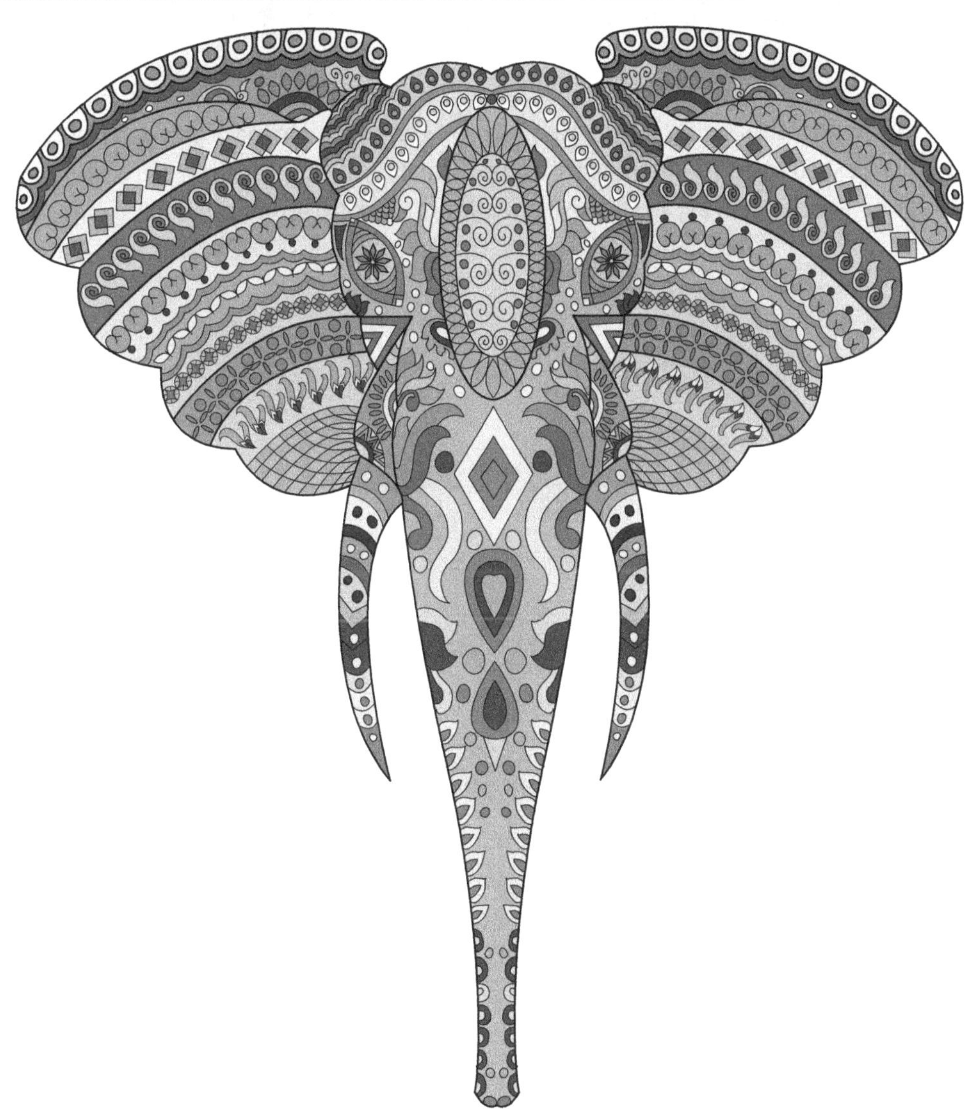

Olivia Tremblay

This Book Belongs To

In a world driven by digital or online communication, media consumption, social habits, and entertainment it can be difficult to find moments in our lives that does not involve screens and scrolling.

This is why perhaps now more than ever we're also seeing an increased need to find technology-free forms of self-care, mindful living, and personal joy. This is precisely why we would like to introduce or reintroduce you to one of the oldest 'tricks of the trade,' coloring. Yes, we are talking good old crayon to paper action—or colored pencils and markers to real-life physical pages of a coloring book.

Considered by some to be a form of moderate art therapy—for children and adults of all ages—studies have shown that allowing yourself to be swept away through the methodical nature and creativity found in coloring, can reduce everyday stresses and anxiety.

Coloring's naturally meditative nature allows one to find easy, present focus. It cultivates creativity, personal expression, and can even provide a feeling of safety and security in an environment controlled by the artist herself!

As our chaotic, distracted mind relaxes, our busy thoughts melt away and we are transported to a land of simple joy. Additional research tells us a habit of coloring can also lead to increased self-awareness and higher levels of self-esteem.

It's time to unplug, unwind, grab your favorite coloring set, and begin

Happy Coloring :)

COLOR TEST PAGE

Animals to Color

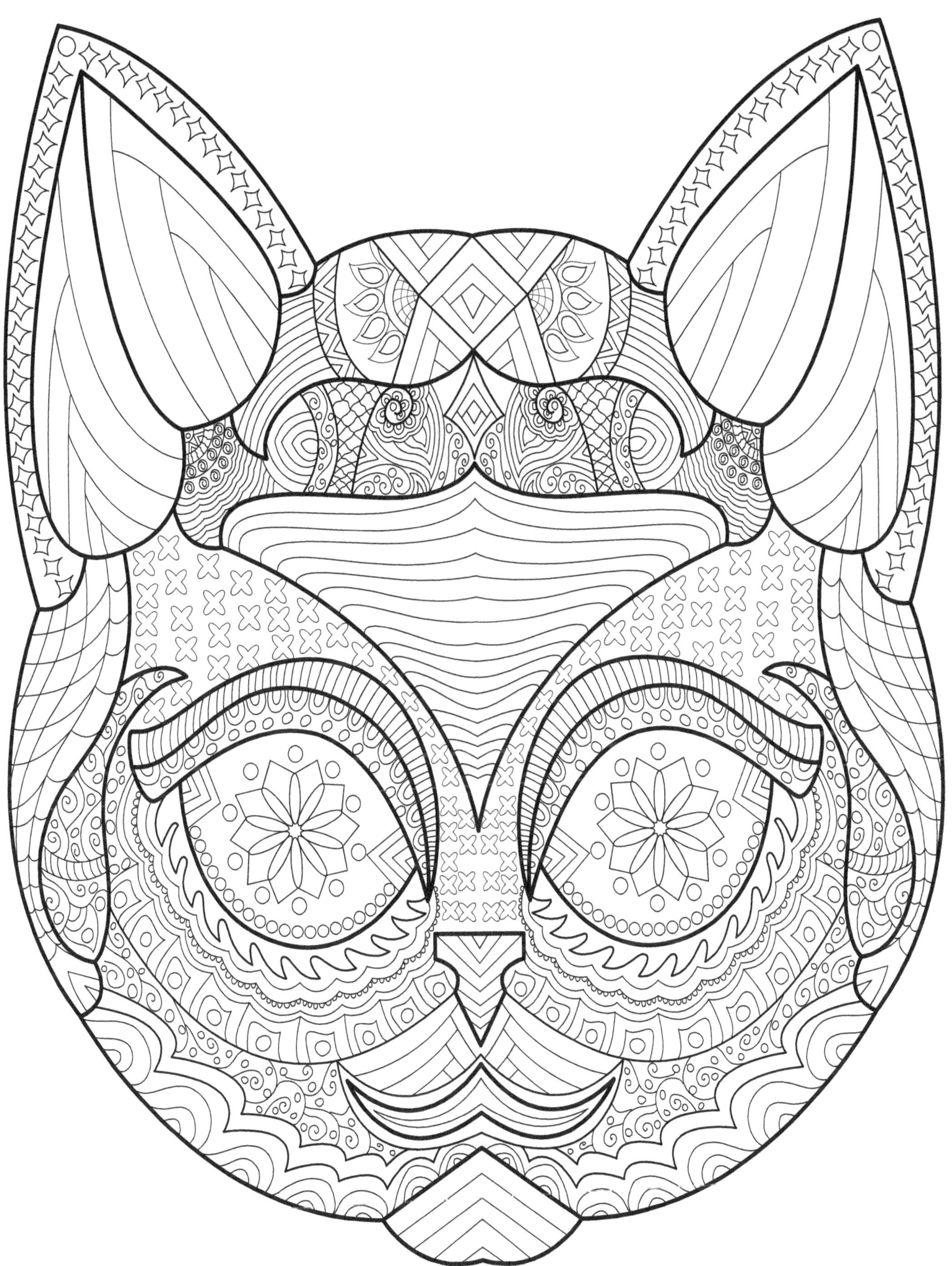

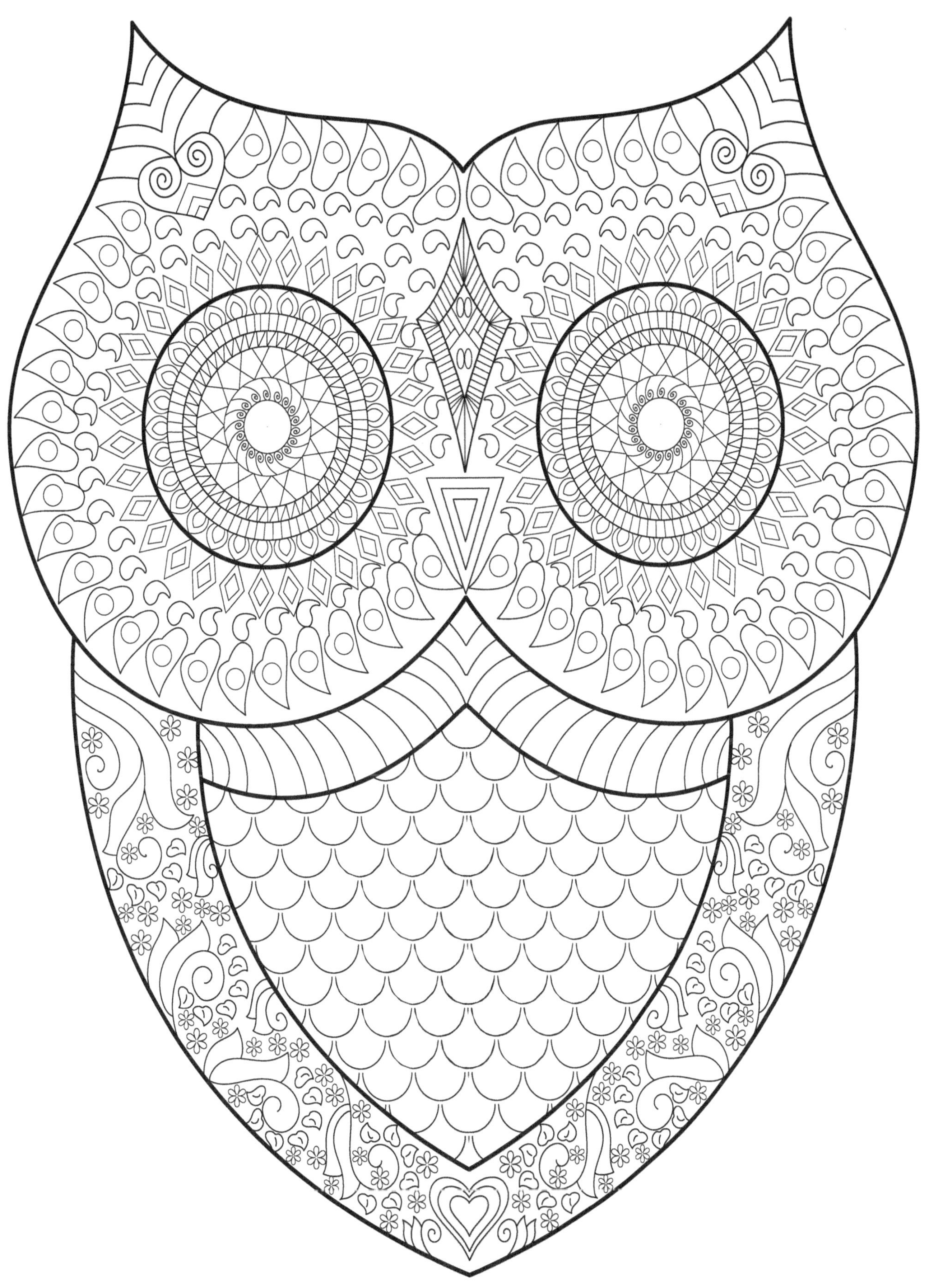

Geometric Patterns

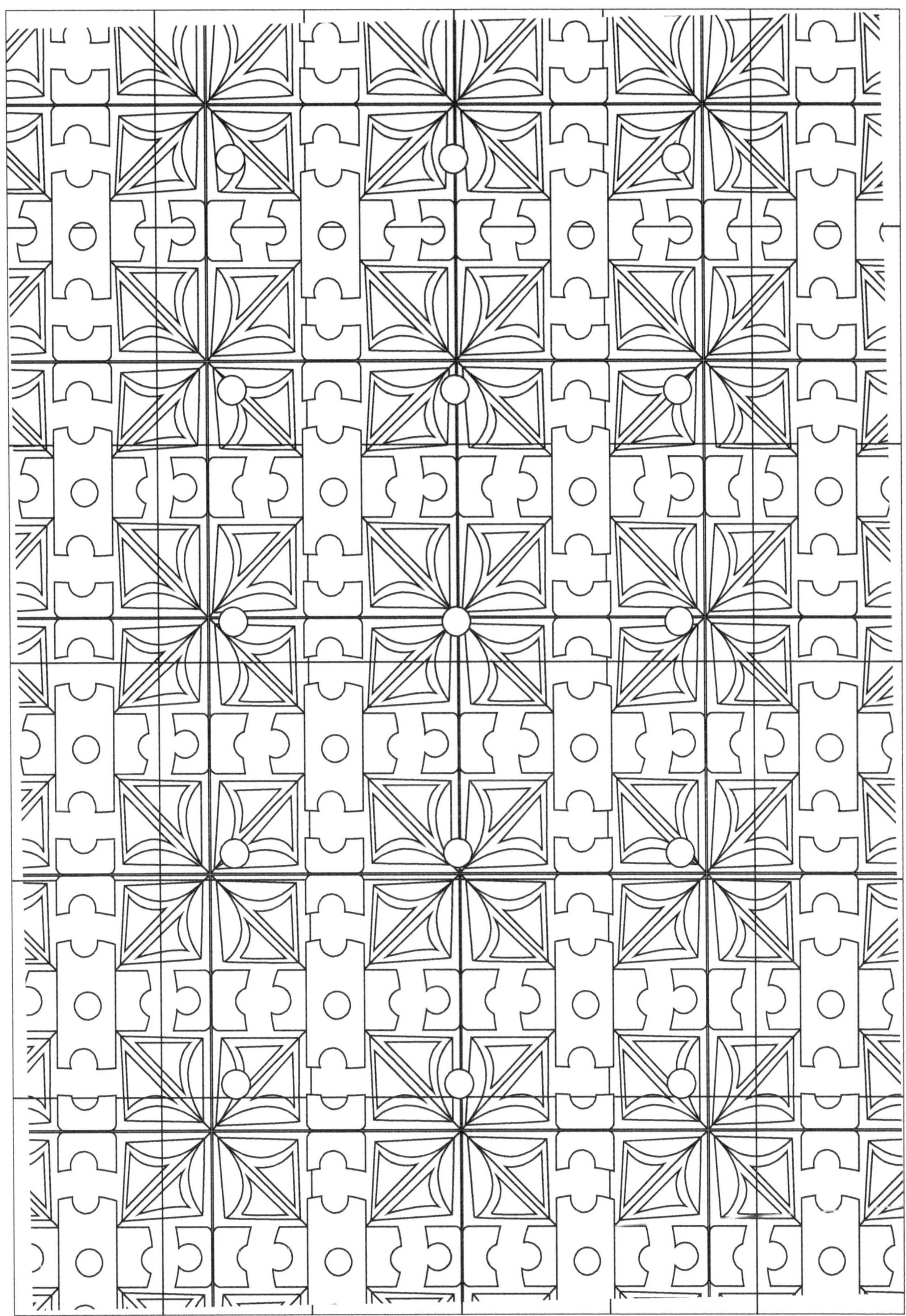

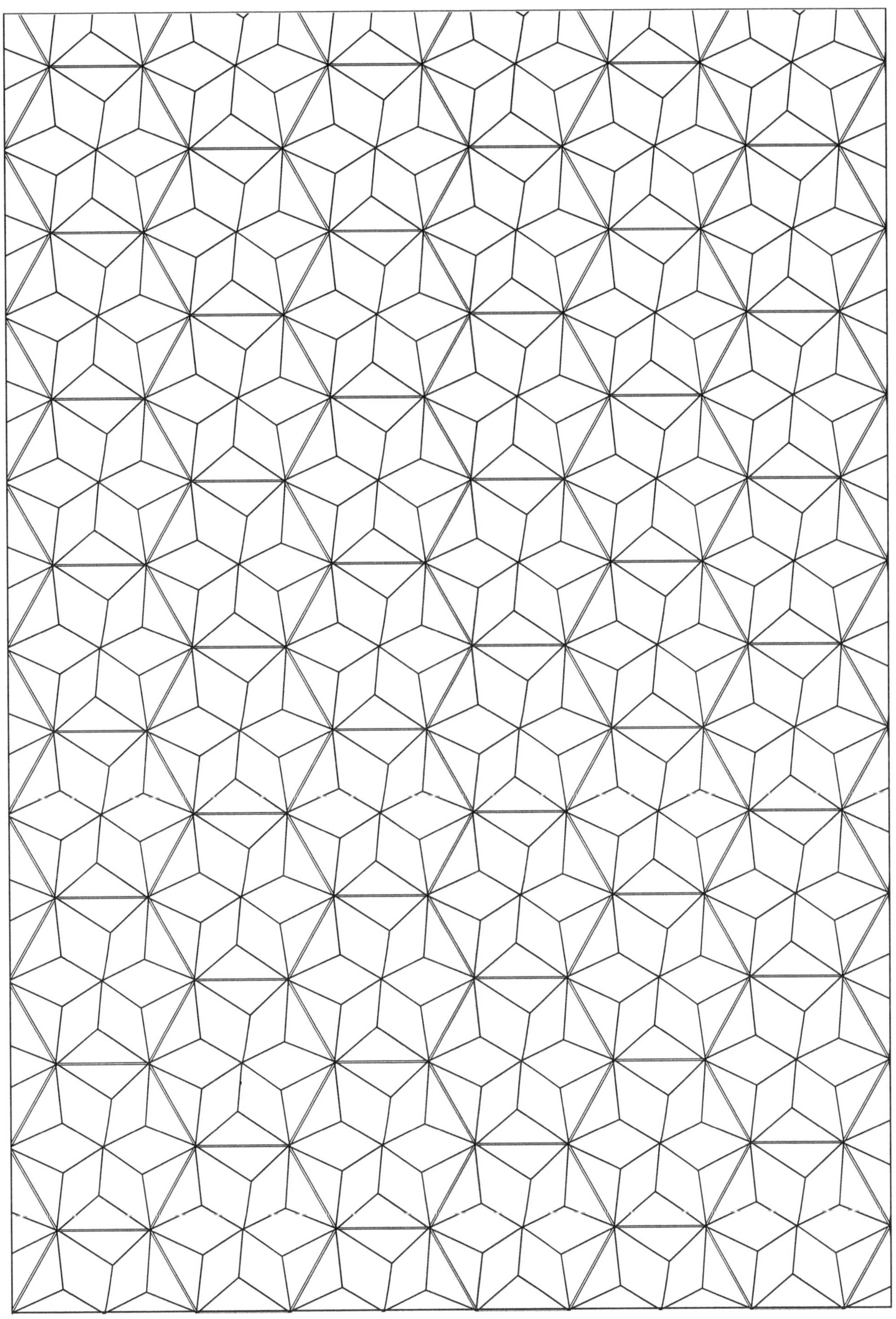

Nature / Flowers

Unicorns / Mermaids

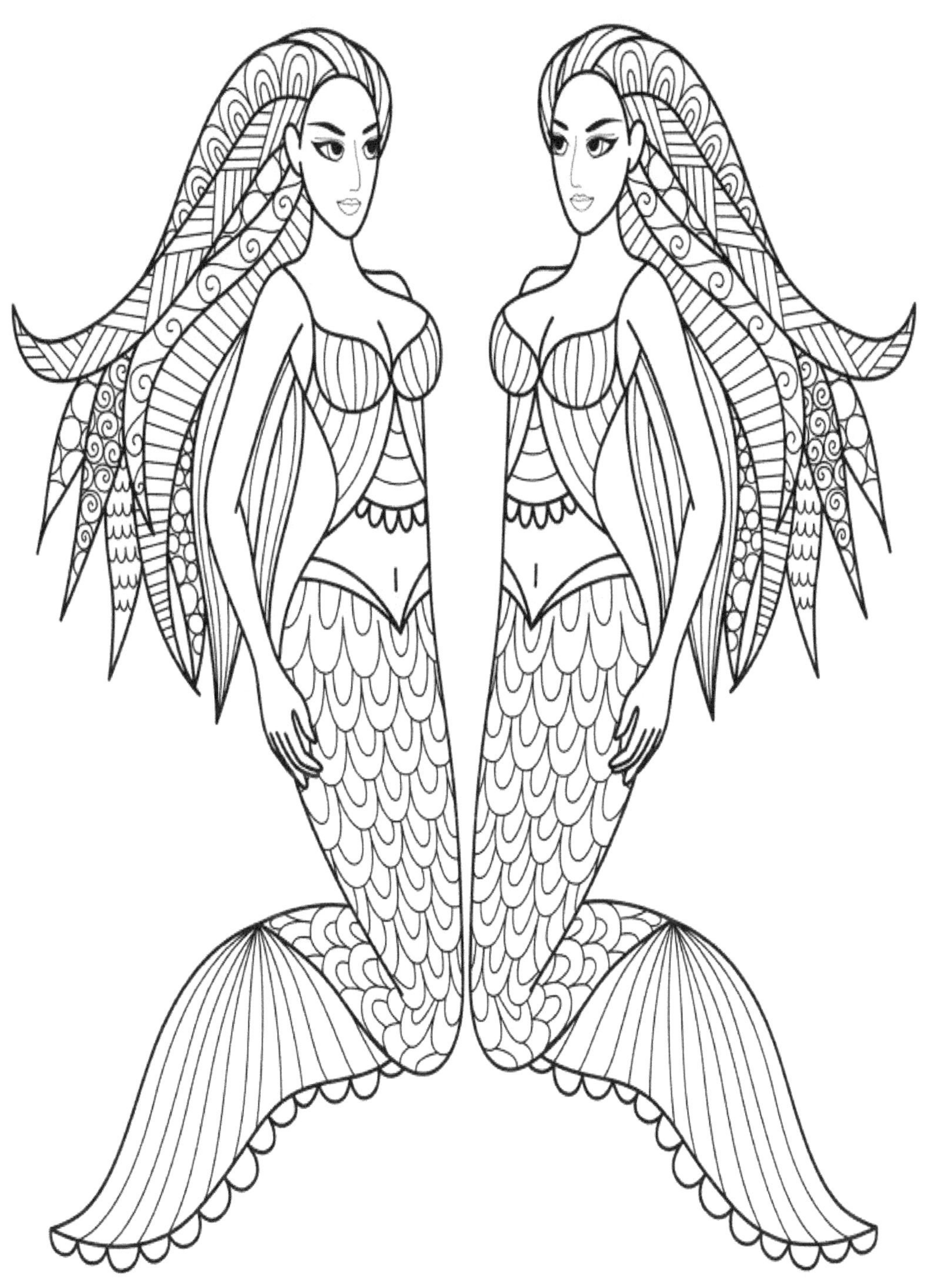

Awesome Mandalas